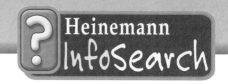

WHY DO I SNEEZE?

✦ and other questions about breathing ✦

Angela Royston

Heinemann Library
Chicago, Illinois

Designed by Joanna Sapwell and StoryBooks
Illustrations by Nick Hawken
Originated by Ambassador Litho
Printed by South China Printers, Hong Kong

07 06 05 04 03
10 9 8 7 6 5 4 3 2 1

J
612.2
ROYS

Library of Congress Cataloging-in-Publication Data
Royston, Angela.
Why do I sneeze? : and other questions about breathing / Angela
Royston.
    p. cm. -- (Body matters)
Includes index.
Summary: Answers common questions about the respiratory system.
  ISBN 1-40340-205-1 (HC)   ISBN 1-40340-460-7 (PB)
  1. Respiratory organs--Juvenile literature. [1. Respiratory system.]
I. Title. II. Series.
  QP121 .R695 2002
  612.2--dc21
                          2002003546

Acknowledgments 3 2530 60562 2149
The author and publishers are grateful to the following for permission to reproduce copyright material:
pp. 5, 7, 8, 9, 15, 23, 28 Gareth Boden; p. 6 Stone; pp. 10, 24 Powerstock Zefa; p. 11 Robert Harding;
pp. 16, 17, 18, 19, 21, 22, 25, 26 Science Photo Library; p. 27 Popperfoto.

Cover photograph by Damien Lovegrove/Science Photo Library.

Every effort has been made to contact copyright holders of any material reproduced in this book.
Any omissions will be rectified in subsequent printings if notice is given to the publisher.

Some words are shown in bold, **like this.** You can find out what they mean by looking in the glossary.

CONTENTS

WHAT HAPPENS WHEN I BREATHE?

When you breathe in, oxygen from the air passes into your lungs and then into your blood. Air containing carbon dioxide leaves your body when you breathe out.

Oxygen is essential for all living things, including humans, animals, plants, and even **bacteria.** When you breathe in, air—a mixture of invisible gases that includes oxygen—is pulled through your nose or mouth, down the **trachea,** to your lungs.

Inside the lungs

The trachea is a wide, tough tube that looks like a vacuum cleaner tube. It divides into two **bronchial tubes,** one for each lung. The bronchial tubes split into many smaller, narrower tubes. At the end of each narrow tube is a cluster of air sacs with lots of tiny **blood vessels** flowing around them. The air sacs

trachea

lung

heart

bronchial tube

blood vessels

alveoli

are called alveoli and each one is like a tiny balloon. As each fills with air, oxygen from the air passes through its thin wall into the blood.

How the body uses oxygen

Blood carries oxygen to the millions of cells that make up your brain, muscles, and bones. Every cell needs energy to do its job. It gets the energy by using oxygen to burn glucose, a kind of sugar, from your food. This produces waste, including carbon dioxide. The waste is transported in the blood until it passes through the walls of the alveoli and joins the air in the lungs. You breathe out this stale air.

The air you breathe out contains some water vapor. If you breathe onto a cold mirror, the water vapor forms mist on the glass.

WHY IS IT HARD TO HOLD MY BREATH FOR LONG?

You can survive for a few days without water, and for a few weeks without food, but you cannot survive for more than a few minutes without **oxygen.** You do not have to think about breathing—your body does it automatically. When you hold your breath, the amount of oxygen in your blood drops, and your body desperately wants to breathe in more air. Soon you are forced to breathe in.

This girl is gasping for air. She has been holding her breath to swim as far as she can underwater.

Healthy lungs

Some people can hold their breath for longer than other people. Swimmers and other athletes have healthy lungs and good breathing muscles. When they breathe in, the air reaches more of their alveoli, so their bodies take in more oxygen with each breath. This means that they can last longer before they have to breathe again.

Yawning

You often yawn when you are tired, or when you are in a stuffy room. Yawning makes you take in a deep breath of air. This provides the brain with extra oxygen to make you more alert.

When your brain is not getting enough oxygen, you begin to feel drowsy. Yawning pulls more air, and more oxygen, into your lungs.

Fainting

The brain needs a lot of oxygen to stay alert. If the brain does not get enough oxygen, you may faint. This means that you lose consciousness. If you feel faint or dizzy, bend forward and put your head between your knees. This brings more blood, and therefore more oxygen, to your brain.

7

WHY DO I SNEEZE?

Sneezing makes something that is irritating the inside of your nose come out of it. Air is made up of gases but it also contains dust, **germs,** and other tiny specks that are mostly too small to see. When you breathe in, some of these tiny specks are pulled into your nose.

Jet of air

The delicate skin inside your nose is protected by a layer of **mucus** that traps dirt and germs. Sometimes a particular speck of dust irritates the lining of your nose, making it itch and tingle. This triggers a sneeze. A strong jet of air rushes from the lungs, down the nostrils. It sweeps mucus and any irritating specks out of the nose.

Grains of pepper make many people sneeze if they breathe them in. Sneezing helps to sweep the grains out of the nose.

Other causes of sneezing

Often, one of the first signs of a cold is sneezing. Colds and flu are caused by germs that you breathe in. If some of these germs get stuck in the lining of your nostrils, you automatically sneeze to clear them away. This helps to get rid of the germs, but make sure that you sneeze into a tissue. Otherwise you may pass the germs to the people around you. Some people are **allergic** to things they breathe in, such as pollen or tiny specks of dust. Their bodies think the specks are harmful germs and they sneeze.

THINGS THAT MIGHT MAKE YOU SNEEZE:

- pepper
- dust
- sunlight
- germs
- pollen, cat hair, mold, or other causes of an allergy

When you sneeze, air rushes down your nose at 70 miles per hour (110 kilometers per hour). That is as fast as a car on the highway.

9

WHY DO I PUFF AND PANT?

The fastest sprinters can run 100 meters on one breath of air. At the end of the race, they are gasping for air.

You puff and pant when your body is desperate for **oxygen.** Panting makes you breathe faster and take in more air with each breath. This quickly provides your body with a large amount of oxygen. As more oxygen gets into your blood, your breathing becomes calmer again.

Exercise

When you breathe normally you only empty and fill about a tenth of your lungs with each breath. When you exercise you breathe deeper and take in more air. Exercise that uses a lot of energy makes you puff and pant. Then you take in about fifteen times the amount of air.

Muscles use oxygen

Exercise means that your muscles are moving your bones. Muscles get their energy by using oxygen to burn glucose, a type of sugar. Glucose comes from food and is brought to the muscles in the blood. The harder the muscles work, the more energy—and the more oxygen—they need.

Red blood cells

Red blood **cells** carry oxygen in the blood. When oxygen becomes attached to a red cell, the cell becomes a brighter color of red. Blood that is low in oxygen is a dark red. About a quarter of the oxygen you breathe in enters your blood. Puffing and panting help attach more oxygen to more red blood cells.

PANTING INCREASES SUPPLY OF OXYGEN

When an adult rests she breathes in about 12 pints (6 liters) of air a minute. When she is sprinting, she breathes in about 190 pints (90 liters) of air a minute—15 times as much as usual.

These children are running as fast as they can. If they keep running like this, they will soon be puffing and panting.

Heartbeat

Exercise that makes you puff and pant also makes your heart beat faster. You can often feel it thudding in your chest. The heart is a pump that pushes blood through the **arteries** and around your body. The faster it beats, the faster blood passes through your lungs, and the faster it picks up **oxygen** to take it to your muscles.

The heart pumps blood to the lungs, where it picks up oxygen. The blood returns to the heart, which then pumps it around the body.

Staying healthy

Regular exercise makes your muscles, heart, and lungs work better. The more you exercise the stronger your muscles become. The heart is a muscle, and exercise makes it stronger too. A strong heart pushes more blood through the arteries with every beat. Healthy lungs take in more oxygen from the air with every breath.

lung

lung

right side of heart pumps blood to lungs

left side of heart pumps blood to body

vein takes blood back to heart

artery

CHILDREN'S LUNGS

A 10-year-old child's lungs hold about 6 pints (3 liters) of air. Children breathe faster than adults—about 20 times a minute, instead of about 15 times a minute for an adult.

When your heart, lungs, and muscles are healthy, you can do much more exercise before you begin to puff and pant.

This woman is climbing a hill. She has to rest every few steps, so she does not lose her breath.

Poor breathing

Unfit people, who do not exercise much, take in only a small amount of air with each breath. They begin to puff and pant easily. People who are overweight also become breathless quickly. Smoking tobacco damages the lungs. Heavy smokers quickly become out of breath. Illnesses, such as **bronchitis,** also affect how well people can breathe.

WHAT ARE HICCUPS?

Hiccups occur when air is suddenly and unexpectedly jerked into your lungs. When you cough, you know that you are going to push air out, but a hiccup often takes you by surprise. Hiccups are caused by a flat sheet of muscle called the diaphragm. It lies underneath your lungs and is the main muscle that you use to breathe in and out.

Your lungs expand and contract as you breathe in and out. The movement is controlled by the diaphragm. A hiccup is caused by a twitch in the diaphragm.

Breathing in and out

Lungs have no muscles of their own. Instead, the diaphragm and the muscles between your ribs control your breathing. To breathe in, the diaphragm moves down, and the ribs move up and out. This creates space in your chest that is filled by air being pulled into your lungs. To breathe out, the diaphragm moves up and the ribs move in. This squeezes air out of the lungs.

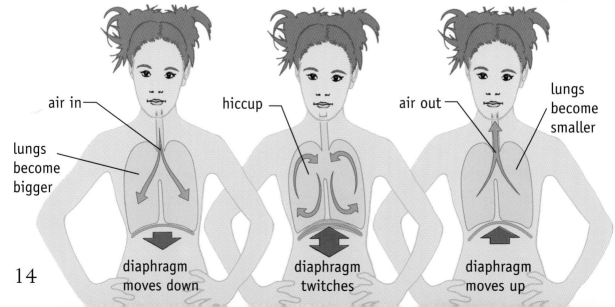

air in

lungs become bigger

hiccup

air out

lungs become smaller

diaphragm moves down

diaphragm twitches

diaphragm moves up

Hiccups

You get hiccups when your diaphragm twitches or jerks downward. This pulls in a gasp of air. At the same time, the top of the **trachea** snaps shut. The air is then forced through the **larynx,** causing the "hic" sound. Different things, including eating lots of fresh bread or spicy food, can cause hiccups. Most cases of hiccups last only a few minutes, but some unlucky people can suffer for days.

This boy is trying to stop his hiccups. Different people have different ways of curing hiccups. You have to find a way that works for you.

POSSIBLE HICCUP CURES:

- holding your breath
- drinking a cup of water from the far side of the cup
- breathing in and out of a paper bag
- sucking sugar

WHAT HAPPENS WHEN I BREATHE POLLUTED AIR?

Polluted air is air that contains specks of dirt, or chemicals from factories, car exhaust, and other sources. Large specks of dirt might make you sneeze but smaller specks pass through your nose or mouth and into your lungs.

Protecting the lungs

The tiny hairs in your breathing tubes look like this under a microscope. They catch dirt and **germs,** and push them back along the tubes out of the lungs.

The **bronchial tubes** and the tubes in your lungs are protected by **mucus** and by very fine hairs. The hairs and mucus trap dust and specks that get into your lungs. The hairs wave backward and forward to push the mucus and the specks out of the lungs.

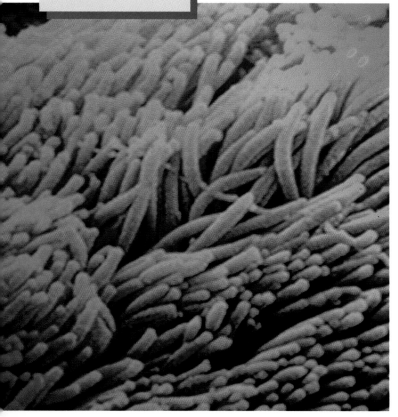

Coughing

If the tubes become clogged with mucus, you cough to clear them. Coughing forces a blast of air through the tubes, **trachea,** and throat to clear them.

Damaging chemicals

Some chemicals stay in the lungs and can damage them. They may irritate the lining of the tubes and make breathing more difficult. If you suffer from **asthma** or **bronchitis,** it is already difficult to breathe. Air pollution makes it worse. Some chemicals can even cause lung cancer.

Ozone

The gas ozone is produced at ground level when sunlight acts on the exhaust fumes of cars, trucks, and other traffic. Breathing air with a lot of ozone can give you a sore throat.

When sunlight combines with traffic fumes it produces ozone and a kind of fog called photochemical smog. It can make your throat sore and irritate your lungs.

THINGS THAT CAUSE AIR POLLUTION:

Outside —
- exhaust fumes from traffic
- waste gases from power stations, oil refineries, factories, and chimneys
- chemical sprays on crops

Inside —
- cleaning materials
- household pest sprays
- paint and glue sprays

Smoking tobacco

Tobacco smoke is one of the most dangerous things that pollute the air. Tobacco smoke contains the gas carbon monoxide and more than 4,000 different chemicals, including the poisons arsenic, hydrogen cyanide, and formaldehyde. Smokers also take in two other damaging substances—tar and nicotine.

Carbon monoxide

Carbon monoxide passes through the lungs into the blood. It attaches itself to red blood **cells** and takes the place of **oxygen** in the blood. This means that there is less oxygen for the brain, heart, and other parts of the body.

The air in this room is polluted with cigarette smoke. Smoke pollution in a room is called secondhand smoke. It can cause lung cancer and other diseases.

Damaging the lungs

Smokers breathe hot gases and chemicals straight into their lungs. The smoke burns their throats and damages the fine hairs and delicate lining of their breathing tubes. The body makes extra **mucus** to try to get rid of the smoke, but smokers' damaged lungs cannot clear the mucus.

Tar and nicotine

Tobacco smoke contains black, sticky tar, like the tar that is used on roads. Over time, the tar clogs the lungs and stops them from working properly. Nicotine is an addictive drug. This means that people who smoke crave the nicotine, and need it for their bodies to work normally.

The healthy lung on the left belonged to a nonsmoker. The lung on the right belonged to a smoker. It is clearly dirty and damaged.

SOME DISEASES CAUSED BY SMOKING:

- bronchitis
- smoker's cough
- emphysema
- lung cancer
- throat and mouth cancer

19

WHY DOES A COLD MAKE MY NOSE BLOCKED?

Inside of the nose, each nostril leads to a nasal passage filled with three shelves of bone. When you have a cold, these passages become clogged with mucus.

Your nose is much bigger than it looks from the outside. Each nostril leads to a passage that contains three shelves of bone. These shelves are lined with **mucus.** When you have a cold, your nose makes extra mucus. The mucus may become so thick that it blocks your nose and makes it harder to breathe.

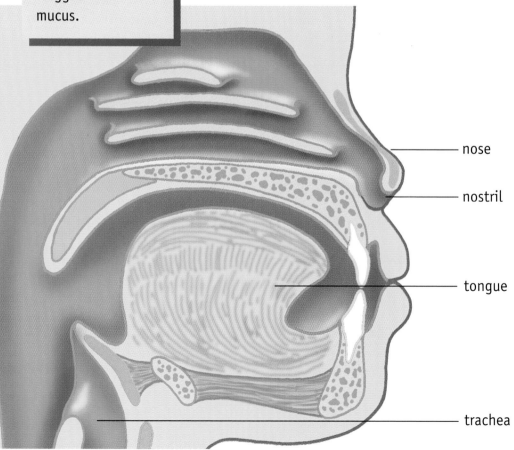

nose

nostril

tongue

trachea

Inflamed and swollen

When you breathe in cold **germs,** they stick in your throat or nose. Germs that stick in your throat make it red and sore. When germs stick in your nose, the passages at the back of your nose become swollen. Your body makes extra mucus to wash the germs away, but the swelling prevents the mucus from escaping.

Fighting germs

Most germs are killed by your body before they have a chance to multiply. Mucus and saliva are antiseptic—that means they help to kill germs—but any germs that survive can multiply quickly. Blood contains white blood **cells**. Their job is to destroy germs. The blood also makes **antibodies** that attack germs.

Getting rid of mucus

Mucus washes away some of the germs. It also washes away dead germs, killed by white blood cells and by antibodies. You get rid of the extra mucus when you blow your nose. Sometimes the mucus becomes so thick with germs it clogs your nostrils. Then you have to breathe through your mouth.

A cold makes your nose run with extra mucus. Even when you blow your nose, the passages soon fill with more mucus.

Cold viruses

Colds are caused by a **virus.** A virus is a particular kind of germ, and there are over 200 different kinds that cause colds. When you have a cold, your body may be invaded by more than one cold virus. One common cold virus is yellow, another one is blue. If your cold is caused by both, the colors of the viruses combine to turn your **mucus** green!

This is what one kind of cold germ looks like under a microscope. Several different viruses can cause a cold.

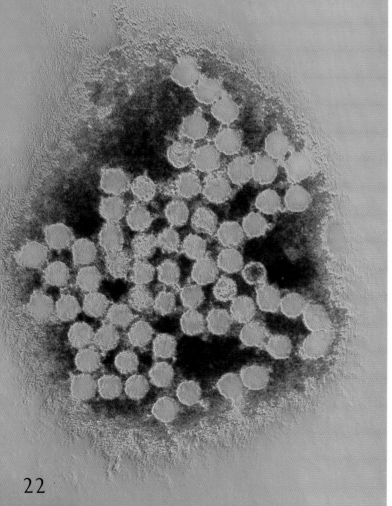

Coughs

Some of the mucus from the nose drains down the throat into the **bronchial tubes.** Colds are often followed by coughs as your body works to clear all the breathing tubes. Sometimes the bronchial tubes become infected by **bacteria** after a cold. Then you suffer from a chest infection. There is no cure for a virus, but the doctor can give you medicine to cure infections that are caused by bacteria.

Sinuses

Sinuses are spaces in the bones of the head and face. They make your skull lighter, so they make it easier for you to hold your head up. These hollows are lined with mucus and are normally filled with air. The mucus drains into the nose.

Sinusitis

When you have a cold, the infection can spread into one or more of the sinuses. Then the sinuses become inflamed and the entrance to the nose becomes blocked. The mucus is trapped in the sinuses. This can make you feel dizzy and give you a painful headache. It can also add to your blocked nose.

Coughing helps to clear your bronchial tubes. Always cover your mouth when you cough. If you do, you will not spread germs to other people.

WHAT MAKES SOME PEOPLE WHEEZE?

People who have **asthma** often wheeze when they breathe. The tubes in their lungs are swollen and narrower than other people's. During an asthma attack the tubes close up and become even narrower. This makes breathing very difficult, and makes it very hard to breathe out. There is often a whistling sound as someone with asthma breathes in, and a wheezing sound as he or she breathes out. Asthma is most common among children.

Allergies often run in families. The girl in this photo has asthma. Her mother has hay fever, and her father has asthma.

Causes of asthma

The most common cause of asthma is an allergy to something such as house dust, pollen, or certain foods. Contact with the thing a person is **allergic** to sets off an asthma attack. An attack can also be triggered by worry or excitement.

An asthma attack

One of the first signs that an attack is about to happen is a feeling of tightness in the chest. The muscles in the **bronchial tubes** tighten up and the lining of the tubes makes extra **mucus.** This makes the tubes so narrow that it is very difficult for air to pass through them. The person becomes breathless and gasps for air, and is unable to breathe properly. Being unable to stop coughing is another early sign of an attack. An attack may last for a few minutes, a few hours, or even several days.

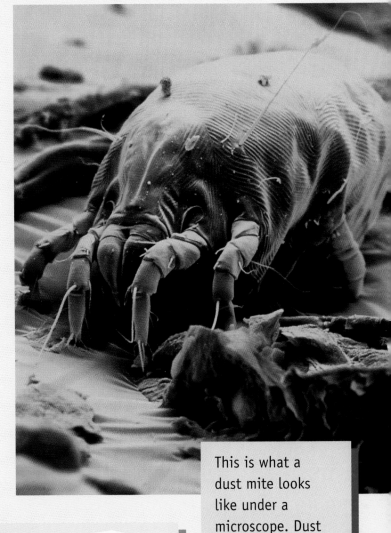

This is what a dust mite looks like under a microscope. Dust mites are too small to see unless they are magnified, but they are a common cause of asthma.

THINGS THAT MAY TRIGGER AN ASTHMA ATTACK:

- tobacco smoke
- pollen
- cold air
- coughs and colds
- pets
- house dust
- exercise
- aspirin

Medicines

There is no cure for **asthma,** but there are medicines that help to control it. Most people with asthma have medicines that they breathe in through an **inhaler.** These drugs make the muscles of the airways relax and open. One medicine helps to relieve an attack. It is taken when the person feels an attack coming on.

This girl is inhaling a drug that will help to prevent her from getting a severe asthma attack.

Another medicine helps to prevent an attack from happening. It has to be inhaled every day.

Treating asthma

An asthma attack can be frightening both for the person having it and for the people with them. It is important that the person with asthma sits down and that everyone stays calm. The person suffering the attack tries to cough the sticky **mucus** up from their lungs.

Once they have coughed mucus out of their lungs, the attack often begins to pass. This makes coughing easier. If the attack does not ease quickly, then you should get medical help.

A normal life

If people with asthma take their medicines, they can do most of the things other people do. They can play games and do other exercise. Most children who suffer from asthma find that their attacks become milder and less frequent as they reach their teens. About half of all children who have asthma will grow out of the condition completely.

Some adults continue to suffer from asthma. Tom Dolan is an Olympic athlete who also has asthma.

WHY DO I HAVE TO STOP TALKING TO BREATHE IN?

You can only talk as you breathe out. Air from your lungs is pushed through the **larynx** in your throat to produce sound. It does not work when you breathe in. The larynx contains two bands of skin called the vocal cords. They vibrate when air passes between them. Muscles stretch and relax the bands to produce different notes. The more relaxed the vocal cords, the lower the note.

You make sounds in the larynx in your throat. If you hold your hand over your throat as you hum, you will feel the voice box vibrate as you make the noise.

Talking and shouting

The larynx produces the note, but you move your lips, tongue, and teeth to make the many different sounds that make up speech. You cannot talk with your mouth shut! To talk louder you have to push a greater amount of air out of your lungs. Before you shout, you need to take in a deep breath of air.

BODY MAP

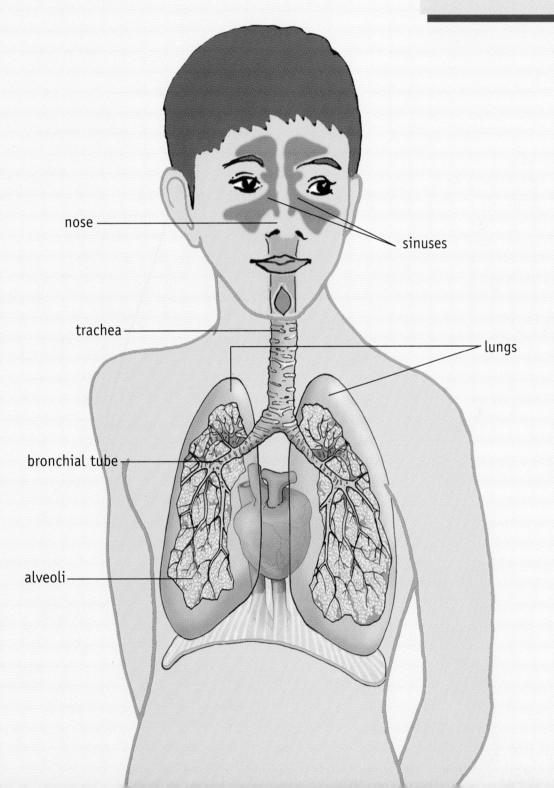

nose

sinuses

trachea

lungs

bronchial tube

alveoli

GLOSSARY

allergic   when the body reacts to something as if it were a germ, even though that thing is harmless to most people

antibodies   cells carried in the blood that attack particular bacteria and viruses

arteries   tubes that blood flows along from the heart to different parts of the body

asthma   condition in which the breathing tubes become inflamed and narrower than usual. This makes it difficult to breathe air into and out of the lungs.

bacteria   tiny living things. Some kinds of bacteria are germs that cause disease.

blood vessels   tubes through which blood moves around the body

bronchial tubes   tubes that join the trachea to the lungs

bronchitis   when the bronchial tubes become inflamed, causing a deep cough

cell   smallest building block of living things. The body has many kinds of cells, including nasal cells, lung cells, and blood cells.

germs   tiny forms of life that can make you ill

inhaler   equipment used to take medicine that must be breathed in

larynx   voice box, that is, the part of the trachea that contains the vocal cords

mucus   slime that coats the inside of parts of the body, including the nose and bronchial tubes

oxygen   gas that living things need to breathe in to survive

trachea   tube that connects the throat to the bronchial tubes

virus   kind of germ that is even smaller than all kinds of bacteria

FURTHER READING

Hardie, Jackie. *Breathing and Respiration*. Chicago: Heinemann Library, 1997.

LeVert, Suzanne. *The Lungs*. Tarrytown, NY: Marshall Cavendish, 2001.

Stille, Darlene. *The Respiratory System*. Danbury, Conn.: Children's Press, 1997.

INDEX